Saving Lives Through Education: Ignite Focus

Book 1 of 3

Dr. Al Thompson

Copyright © 2020 by Al Thompson

All rights reserved.

ISBN 978-1-62806-270-0

Library of Congress Control Number 2020915083

Published by Salt Water Media
29 Broad Street, Suite 104
Berlin, MD 21811
www.saltwatermedia.com

Cover design by Beth Anne Sonberg-Thompson

No part of this book may be reproduced without the permission of the author.

To learn more, visit: www.savinglivesinc.com

The *Saving Lives Through Education* Series
shares one man's journey
from firefighter to educator
and highlights instructional strategies
that have the greatest positive impact
on student achievement.

This is Book 1 of the series:
IGNITE FOCUS

To My Bride, Beth:

Our first date was April 26, 1980. Anything good that's happened to me, since that day, is because of you. Through loss of jobs, loss of our home during Hurricane Isabel, and my Parkinsons, daily you model love and the insignificance of material possessions. You are my lighthouse! You are amazing. Thank you.

To Beth, Becky, Sarah, Dot, and Ed ...

Thank you for your unconditional love and support!

Acknowledgements

In the spring of 2016, I was diagnosed with Parkinson's disease. After the initial shock, there were times when I wondered if I would ever be able to complete this project, *Saving Lives Through Education: Ignite Focus*. I'd like to acknowledge the following people in my life who have been responsible for pushing me every day to continue my mission and "Never, never, never give up!" (W. Churchill):

Dan O'Connor	Mark Ciarapica
Tim Cahill	Chris Massoni
Lawrence Daniels	Greg Massoni
Cheryl Dunkle	Primo
Todd Fishburn	Paul J. Redmond
Kay and Chuck LaHatte	Doug Reeves
Billy Lupinacci	Teodora
Tommy Thompson	

And a very special thanks to **Ann Fontaine Lewis** and **Susan Nancarrow**, whose dedication to the writing and the publication of my story helped make it a reality! Their tireless efforts and the countless hours they devoted to planning, researching, organizing, writing, and editing have made the *Saving Lives Through Education* series possible.

Table of Contents

First Alarm 15

Second Alarm 19

Third Alarm 29

Strategic & Intentional Action Strategy to Ignite Focus 43

References 45

About the Author 47

A Preview of *Book 2: Fuel Feedback* 49

Note: The chapter titles, "First Alarm," "Second Alarm," and "Third Alarm," refer to the practice of fire companies referring to emergency situations based on their increasing urgency, intensity, and need for action. For example, when the "First Alarm" is called, a fire company in a particular jurisdiction might immediately send out four engines, two trucks, and a chief. As each subsequent alarm is called, additional equipment and personnel is sent out – hence, terms such as "four-alarm fire." The urgency, intensity, and need for action to save the lives of our children through education parallel those factors in the firefighting profession.

*Saving Lives Through Education:
Ignite Focus*

First Alarm

Since my career in education began, I have spoken openly and enthusiastically about my previous experiences as a firefighter with the Baltimore City Fire Department and the parallels of saving lives in the two professions. Those conversations have inevitably provoked many questions from both adults and children: What was it like to put your life on the line each day as a firefighter, in the service of complete strangers? What prompted you to leave a successful career to which you were totally committed, in exchange for one that would require years of additional education and training? What skills and insights did you gain as a firefighter that you now bring to the teaching profession? Do you find the same type of fulfillment in education that you did through firefighting?

Often, the answers to those questions have stimulated additional questions – ones such as: How do the challenges of firefighting parallel the challenges in education today? How can our actions as educators mimic those of first responders in emergency situations? What life experiences have led you to your insights and to this calling that drives you both personally and professionally?

In preparing to write this book, I have reflected long and hard about these questions and others like them.

To share the journey that has brought me to a life of service to others and to the purpose that drives my daily mission to save lives through education requires that you know some key information about my background. As a child, I was not on the stereotypical track to becoming a successful professional devoted to saving lives through firefighting or education, or frankly, to having any career at all.

On the contrary, I was headed in the opposite direction. As the third of four children born to parents with an eighth grade education, education was not a priority in our home. Struggling daily to make ends meet, my father supported my family by working two jobs – making him frequently absent from my life. My mother didn't know what she didn't know about parenting, but did the best she could. I learned early on that growing up with both parents didn't necessarily guarantee a perfect childhood. As a result of the dysfunction in my home, from an early age I ran the streets of Baltimore City, learning the lessons offered by that kind of life. Those street lessons, plus the daily, often painful experiences of parochial school convinced me that education was not for me. I was quickly on track for a life that could only end with bad news.

Somehow, though, I began to emerge from the dark challenges and inadequacies of my formative years, taking advantage of possibilities that, at first, seemed very foreign to me. Although a long time coming, the first possibility offered itself during my senior year in high school. The cliques in school and resulting divisions among my peers had always bothered me. My goal was for everybody to get along – all of the groups within our school culture. I remember thinking that I wanted everyone to enjoy our last year together in school, so I decided that I would contradict the prevailing expectations of me, both at home and at school, and run for Senior Class President. And it happened – I won the election! The whole experience confirmed my growing confidence in myself. So,

I thought, those other kids I had perceived as having such different futures than I, did not have the corner on dreams and happiness, after all.

That experience paved the way for more possibilities down the road; however, the transformation would happen slowly, with a lot of challenges still ahead. After high school graduation and a year of continuing to enjoy the streets of the city, on a whim I took the firefighter exam and was accepted into the academy, beginning my calling as a firefighter at age eighteen. Four years later, I became the youngest lieutenant in Baltimore City Fire Department history. Even with those milestones though, the challenges of my youth would continue to bring ups and downs in my life for some time. No one would have predicted the path that would eventually lead me to a doctorate in education twenty-five years later, or to the mission that now drives my life's work and provides the focus of this book.

At this point in my educational career, I have come to the realization that sharing my life experiences and the insights I have gained as a result might help others see the promise in themselves and in all children. I want nothing more than for every teacher to realize that no matter what challenges a child might face, in and out of school – or what challenges the child might present for others; there are always strategies for encouraging that child to take steps toward a positive and productive future. As a teacher, you are in a position to help students find their way toward that future, a future that could very well save their lives. My goal for this book is to ignite a fire in the soul of every educator in America, a fire that sparks a career-long commitment to making a difference in each child's life, daily. As military strategist Ferdinand Foch (n.d.) said, "The most powerful weapon on earth is the human soul on fire." *Saving Lives Through Education* is the series that will forever change the way you think about your true mission in teaching – the mission of saving lives.

Second Alarm

April 1987
Firefighter Lieutenant
Baltimore City, Maryland

I sat in the Baltimore City Fire Department doctor's office, absorbing what he had just told me.

"You don't work here anymore," he had said.

Not believing the words, I had responded, "What do you mean?"

"Your papers are at the pension office. Go to City Hall, Room #410, and talk to somebody."

- **1,523,635 firefighters were injured on the job between 1981 and 2012.**
- **An estimated 58,250 firefighters were injured in the line of duty in 2018.**

Somehow, I made it outside. I felt like I couldn't breathe. My first thought was to call my wife.

When she answered, I took a deep breath. The only thing that would come out of my mouth was, "Beth..." Then I forced the doctor's message through my lips, *"They don't want me anymore."*

Without a pause, she said, "I love you. And I will always want you. Come on home."

On the way home, it hit me like a ton of bricks. It's over. The last fourteen years flew through my head: saving lives every day. . . , the intense rush of the work . . . , the relationships built. . . . , the friends lost on the job . . . , the funerals attended . . . , the accidents and tragedies experienced . . . , the kids saved – the kids . . . .

- 1,594 firefighters were killed on the job from 1981 to 2012.
- 96 firefighters (career, volunteer, municipal) were killed on the job in 2018.
- The average number of children age 14 and under killed by fire each year is 3,650.
- Every day, at least one child dies from a home fire and another 293 are injured from fires or burns.
- Each year, nearly 488 children ages 14 and under die in home fires and another 116,600 children are injured from a fire/burn related incident.

I opened the door to find my wife waiting for me. I searched her eyes for a reaction.

"What am I gonna do when I grow up?" I asked.

She smiled. "You would make a great school teacher!"

I looked at her, shocked at the suggestion.

"You love helping people, and that's what teachers do."

- 91% of teachers say that they came in to teaching because of a desire to help children.
- Almost all teachers join the profession because of a "desire to impact people's lives."
- Among top survey results regarding why a particular teacher made a difference in a person's life was, "They imparted life lessons as well as academic lessons."
- 46% of new teachers leave the profession within 5 years.

- *Each year, more than 200,000 teachers leave the profession with nearly two out of three leaving for reasons other than retirement.*

May 1993
Middle School English Teacher
Baltimore City, Maryland

I had been a middle school English teacher in a Baltimore City middle school for two years when I first met Henry Flynn. He was a student with a visual impairment assigned to my third period class. The makeup of my eighth grade class included kids from low-income neighborhoods and the inner city projects, some of the same neighborhoods I had served as a firefighter. Every day I was reminded of the multitude of challenges they faced.

"Tap, tap, tap ..." The sound of Henry's Braille typewriter was a constant backdrop to the interaction in my classroom. Henry's classmates were used to the sound; it never distracted them. They were among Henry's strongest supporters.

- *The number of students, ages 3-21 in 2017-2018, who received special education services under the Individuals with Disabilities Education Act (IDEA) was 7 million or 14% of all public school students. Among students receiving special education services, 34% had specific learning disabilities.*

Henry lived with his parents in one of the inner city neighborhoods served by the school. Unlike many of his peers, he did not lack the vocabulary and skills expected of most eighth graders. His thirst for learning was tangible. His confidence in his own potential surmounted the challenges of his blindness.

I interacted with Henry, as I did with my other students, communicating high expectations and my enthusiasm for their success in learning. Sometimes, I would get carried away in my own excitement.

"Slow down, Mr. Thompson," Henry called out, as he worked conscientiously to capture his notes in Braille.

Henry would call me at home on evenings and weekends to ask about an assignment or to talk about an idea we had explored in class. His perseverance inspired me when I was exhausted by the daily demands of teaching.

- **The effect size of student expectations as an influence on achievement is 1.33.**
- **The effect size of teacher-student relationships as an influence on student achievement is 0.52.**[1]

As an end-of-the-year trip, our eighth graders were treated to a day at an amusement park. It was pouring rain. Henry was my partner for the day, and we had covered ourselves with garbage bags as makeshift rain ponchos. Henry was game for anything! His hand on my shoulder, we headed to one of the

---

[1] "An **effect size** of 0.40 sets a level where the effects of innovation enhance achievement in such a way that we can notice real-world differences." An **effect size** for a strategy which is less than 0.40 "... can be regarded as in need of more consideration..." (Hattie, 2009).

water rides. As our turn came, I looked into the dugout log where we were about to sit.

"It's filled with water, Henry!" I warned.

Henry quipped, "Mr. Thompson, just be quiet and lead me."

Henry's unconditional faith in me set me back on my heels. In that moment, I discovered my mission – to make a difference in the lives of my students.

- *The effect size of teacher credibility as an influence on achievement is 0.90.*

October 2004
High School Principal
Baltimore City, Maryland

I opened the Sunday newspaper and the headline jumped out at me:

FIVE TEENS SHOT – TWO DEAD

I had a sick feeling in my stomach. My first thought was, "Are any of them our kids?" I found myself anticipating a call from District Office.

I read on. No names were given because of their ages. I kept reading. Then I came to the street address of the location of the crime. It was in one of the neighborhoods served by the high school where I now served as Principal!

According to an interview with the family member of a student from our school, his mother had dropped her son off at a neighboring house while she went out for the evening. Unknown to her, several teenaged dropouts living in that house were affiliated with one of the city's gangs. In the middle of the night, rival gang members, intent on settling a grudge, had burst into the house and opened fire. The boy from our school had been asleep on the sofa. Now, he was among the casualties.

I had just finished reading the article when the phone rang.

- *511,468 students (9th – 12th graders) dropped out of public schools in the United States in 2009-10.*
- *Every year, over 1.2 million students drop out of high school in the United States alone. That's a student every 26 seconds- or 7,000 a day.*
- *Between October 2015 and October 2016, the number of 15- to 24-year-olds who left school without obtaining a high school credential was approximately 532,000.*
- *1,982 juveniles (ages 10-19) were murdered in the United States in 2010.*

July 2012
Leadership Coach
Sussex County, Delaware

Driving along the cornfield-lined road, my mind grappled

with what I was experiencing. After several years as principal in urban and suburban settings, I had most recently been working with the principals of five rural and suburban schools, all of whom served high poverty communities with similar demographics and challenges. As a leadership coach, I was tasked with helping to develop the leadership skills of each of the principals so they could successfully lead their schools to consistently high performance teaching and learning.

Over the previous year, I had gotten to know the principals, their staffs, and their students. I was struck by how similar, and yet how different their situations were.

For months, I had been tailoring my coaching to the specific needs of each principal and each school; as a result, I found myself always returning to the obvious – a research-proven truth – the effectiveness of classroom teaching and learning.

As I walked the halls of Bayside Elementary School, I stopped to visit a classroom during Response to Intervention time. Students were working in small groups around the room and hallway. I saw Miguel, who had just arrived from Cuba earlier in the week, talking in Spanish with an interpreter about a book they were reading in class. He was oblivious to the activity around him, totally committed to meeting the expectations of the adult working with him. Around the room, other students were working in differentiated groups on different tasks. Some students were working individually with support from the other adults circulating around the room. Everyone in the classroom, adults and children alike, were focused on the learning process.

- *The effect size of* **Response to Intervention** *as an influence on achievement is 1.21.*

- *... When **focus** is combined with other variables ... student achievement gains are more than five times greater ..."* (Reeves, 2010).

Here I was in the middle of this great opportunity to work with several schools simultaneously – schools with the same economic background, the same ethnic diversity, the same challenges. Continually, I was reminded of the common focus of the most successful schools among the group – a laser-like focus on a culture devoted to teaching and learning.

October 2012
Leadership Coach
Sussex County, Delaware

Visitors in a classroom at Reliance Elementary noticed that the teacher in the room seemed particularly skilled in encouraging students to focus on their learning tasks for the lesson. Throughout the room were visual prompts to support student learning, as well as resources for meeting a variety of student needs. It was apparent that there was not a student in the room who wasn't engaged in meeting the expectations for active learning.

One visitor leaned over and asked Kaitlyn, one of the nine-year olds in the classroom, who was absorbed in responding to a writing prompt, "How's your work going?"

Kaitlyn look up and said, without reservation, "Great!"

The visitor asked out of curiosity, "How do you know you're doing so well?"

With confidence and a bit of an air of impatience with the visitor's lack of understanding, Kaitlyn responded, "I'm doing everything that we learned and that this rubric reminds me to do! See that example over there on the wall? Go read it and then read the one I've written. You can see that I'm doing great!"

Impressed, the visitor walked over to the teacher and inquired, "How long have you been teaching here?"

"Oh, I'm not a teacher," she said. "I'm the substitute in this classroom today."

- *The effect size of teacher clarity on student achievement is 0.75.*[2]
- *The effect size of student awareness of the learning process (metacognitive strategies.) is 1.33.*[3]

It had been an eventful journey from firefighter to leadership coach – one full of unexpected challenges, highs and lows, and surprising lessons along the way. There is one thing I feel certain of today: as an educator, no less than when I was a firefighter, I have had daily opportunities to save lives. Throughout the years since I made the change in professions, I have had opportunities to save lives each and every day.

---

2 Hattie defines teacher clarity quoting the (unpublished) work of Fendick (1990) as "organization, explanation, examples and guided practice, and assessment of student learning—such that clarity of speech was a prerequisite of teacher clarity." (Hattie 2009, 126) One of the main points of Hattie's books about Visibile Learning is the importance to clearly communicate the intentions of the lessons and the success criteria. Clear learning intentions describe the skills, knowledge, attitudes and values that the students needs to learn. Teachers need to know the goals and success criteria of their lessons, know how well all students in their class are progressing and know where to go next. https://visible-learning.org/glossary/#9_Teacher%20clarity
3 Hattie defines collective efficacy as "a group's shared belief in the conjoint capabilities to organize and execute the courses of action required to produce the given levels of attainment." 1.57

I have felt the intense rush of the work. I have treasured the relationships built. I have experienced funerals, accidents, and tragedies among my students. I have lamented those I have lost. But in the end, my work has been continually ignited by those lives I have been able to save every day.

My wife was right – as she always is. I love this profession! Saving lives through education has become my life's mission.

Third Alarm

December 1979
Fire Lieutenant
Baltimore City, Maryland

As we rolled-up on New Year's Eve, fire was blowing out of every front window of the three-story row house. The street was overflowing with hysterical neighbors screaming frantically, "There are children in there!"

It was New Year's Eve, 1979, and I had volunteered to switch shifts at work that night because one of the married guys had plans with his family. The typical banter among men in a firehouse on an uneventful night spread through the kitchen as the guys used any excuse to rib each other. Pudi Lewis stood overseeing a pot of chili that sat nearly ready on the stove; the smell of still-warm cornbread called our names.

Earlier, we had responded to a couple of false alarms and a report of a dumpster fire -- nothing significant. Things were slow, but as we listened to the sounds of celebratory gunfire around the neighborhood, we knew that the calm would be short-lived.

It was 11:30 p.m. We heard the intercom click on, and dispatch immediately reported a house engulfed in flames in the 500 block of N. Carrollton Avenue. Within seconds, the brass gongs were reverberating throughout the firehouse, calling us to duty. And then we were on 13 Engine rolling out of the station. Adrenalin raced through our bodies as the truck howled through the streets, sirens blaring full blast. Each of us was wondering... *How many people are trapped? Are they old?*

Are they young? What will it take to save them? We were focused on harnessing our energy; everything we had trained for, everything we had rehearsed a thousand times was running through our heads. Then dispatch radioed, "Attention all units responding to the 500 block North Carrollton. We have reports of several children trapped." We looked at each other and without hesitation, or even words, we nodded in silent agreement, "Let's roll!"

As we arrived on the scene, fire was blowing out of every front window of the three-story row house. The street was overflowing with hysterical neighbors screaming frantically, "There are children in there!" Like a Roman candle on the fourth of July, the burning house seemed to rise out of the middle of an entire strip of identical, attached residences on the block. Men, women, and children in their night clothes poured out of the other homes into the streets – some stood paralyzed and silent; others ran panic-stricken from one to another as the fire engulfed the once, seemingly insignificant location.

As we approached, we saw another company already pulled up to the front of the house. Because we were second to arrive, we swung into the trash-filled alley and careened around to the rear of the blazing building. A third engine was approaching from the other direction, driving directly toward us. I radioed to them to cover the rear with their hoses, and we would go in for the rescue. Ultimately, four trucks were on the fireground, with twenty-five firefighters, four of those pump operators, and a battalion chief barking orders.

Urgently, I analyzed the situation from ground level. Then I saw the challenge -- the door and windows in the back of the house were barricaded with burglar bars, the iron rails intended to keep others out, now keeping us from the innocent lives inside. I quickly scanned the entire rear section of the building; just above the barred door and windows was a short porch roof. At first glance, there seemed no way to access it. Then I saw the possibility. I ran up the staircase to the deck of the adjacent house, climbed up the porch railings, and launched myself across to the adjoining roof of the burning row house, losing my helmet in the process. I had no sooner managed to gain my footing, than the third floor windows exploded above my head. The force sent shattering glass in my direction; flames and smoke billowed out. At that moment, I didn't realize how badly I had been cut.

Just steps behind me, my comrade Ray Puckett, recognizing my intention, had followed me up on to the porch roof, and had somehow grabbed my helmet as it fell. As he handed over my helmet, I grabbed it and swung with all the force I had, breaking through the glass of a second floor window; then, using the full weight of my body, I kicked in the frame. We crawled through . . . into the inferno.

Knowing that 8 Engine was at the front of the house strategically pouring water with their hoses, trying to quell the spreading devastation, I yelled to Ray, "Let's find 'em! You get this room," signaling to him that I would move on to the next room.

As I charged my way through the flames and dense smoke, I searched vigorously for the children, praying to locate even one. As the company entering the front of the house targeted their hoses toward the ceilings which created a spray over the room, I strategically continued searching for any of the seven trapped within the incinerating walls. Finally, reaching, I felt one -- a small child, perhaps a year old, huddled under a bed.

I scooped him up, immediately working to breathe life into his tiny body. He seemed to weigh nothing in my arms. The engine company continued the deluge of water over the other rooms on that floor. There was yelling and screaming and nothing but smoke, flames, and debris. Then, out of the chaos, I caught a glimpse of Ray, carrying a second child, and we were both forging ahead, down the steps, through the smoke and flames, and through the firefighters who were making their way in. Other firefighters not far behind us emerged with additional children, rescued.

Continuing my frantic efforts to resuscitate the child in my arms, I stumbled into the open air. Mouth-to-mouth, I swaddled him protectively. My one overriding thought was, "Get him air! Get him air!" Even as the child's lips melted into mine, I could only distantly hear the voices trying to tell me, "Lieutenant, Lieutenant..." Glancing up, I saw blood everywhere. Two of my fellow firefighters grabbed me; one looked me directly in the eyes and said, "Look, he's gone." It wouldn't register. I relentlessly continued my efforts to bring him back to life. Intently, a brother focused my eyes on the life-ending injuries of the child – so obvious, but evidence I had refused to acknowledge until then. A life so brief, now lost.

A medic raced over and forced me to the ground, ordering me to lie down and remain still. Reluctantly dropping to the pavement, I handed the child's limp body over to another firefighter. As the medic bandaged my head, the images flooded back -- my helmet falling, the windows exploding, the glass shattering . . . The blood I saw and thought was the child's, had been mine. It seemed as if an eternity had passed, and yet only minutes had gone by.

Amid the chaos of sirens, radios transmitting calls for assistance, barking of orders, screaming and wailing of family; ambulances were everywhere. Seven had responded to the call to transport the children. After the seventh one pulled out with the last child, another ambulance from a distant part of the city arrived. My head still bleeding, one of the paramedics onboard saw me and insisted on further addressing my injuries. Then he said to his partner, "We're heading to the hospital." When I heard the other EMT, a rookie, say, "I don't know how to get there," I realized neither of the two were familiar with the area or the neighborhoods between North Carrollton Avenue and Greene Street, the location of University Hospital. I assured them I could drive myself there, to the Shock Trauma Center, although my offer demonstrated more "con" than confidence.

A shaved head and twenty-three stitches later, I arrived back at the firehouse. Reluctantly, I was packing up to go home for the remainder of my fourteen-hour shift. As I left, the guys pointed to my stitches and chided, "You'd do anything to get off on New Year's Eve." With a bravado I didn't feel, I rolled my eyes and headed toward my truck in the firehouse parking lot. Innocence forever lost weighed heavily on my mind and in my heart.

All seven children had been pulled unconscious from the inferno, rescued by the men of various Baltimore City fire companies. Five were resuscitated successfully. Their mother had left them alone to go up the street to the corner store for cigarettes; the other adults in the house had been further down the street at a party. With candles lit throughout the house, one of the children on the first floor had apparently knocked a candle over while the other children slept, unaware of the impending tragedy.

Still horrifically and permanently etched in my mind from that New Year's Eve call are the fight through the fire, the suffocating smoke, the relentless search, and the tragic loss of someone's child, brother, or sister. Although many would say we should feel gratified knowing that we had managed to save five, how could we have celebrated when we knew we had lost two? Over the years since, unexpected reminders have repeatedly re-ignited the agonizing moments of that night.

In the conflagration and chaos of that New Year's Eve, with seven children trapped in the firestorm of a Baltimore row house, we responded strategically and intentionally. Our focus was on one thing, and one thing only – saving the lives of those children.

April 1992
Middle School English Teacher
Baltimore City, Maryland

You could have heard a pin drop in the room. All eyes were on Richard and me. I knew this was the moment that would change everything – for Richard and for the rest of the class.

It was the beginning of the 1992-93 school year at the inner city middle school where I was teaching eighth grade

English Language Arts when I first met Richard. He came with the reputation of "psycho" from the staff who had previously dealt with him. Even his peers expected Richard to erupt at the slightest provocation. Nothing Richard did surprised them – at least nothing, yet.

On the first day of school, he and I had a "man-to-man" conversation before he came into the classroom. I was feeling rather smug that I had successfully communicated my expectations to him with apparent success.

However, my perceived success was short-lived. Seven seconds after our conversation, he was out of control! Not yet even settled into a seat, he had sauntered over to one of the other students who was taking supplies out of his backpack. Without any forewarning, Richard grabbed that student's notebook, ripped out a handful of pages, simultaneously demanding, "Gimme a piece a paper!"

The other students in the class froze, waiting for my reaction. My eyes searched the room for Dan who had been in the eighth grade for three years, and in my classroom for two of those years. I knew I could count on him to help me focus Richard. I winked at him and said, "Dan, I'm putting you in charge of Richard." Dan walked over and, using his good nature and considerable size, managed to encourage Richard to a seat; then he sat down at the desk next to him. Meanwhile, I picked up a stack of loose-leaf paper on my desk and delivered it to the boy whose notebook had been assaulted.

I began distributing the literature books that students would be using in our class all year. They were large, heavy, hardbacked volumes that had seen better days. I directed students to write their names in the designated place in the front of the book, while I called out their names to take attendance and get the numbers of their books for my inventory. They responded to their names by yelling out their book numbers – along with the jabs and insults they typically had for each other. I could tell that it was going to be a challenging year with this group. Most of them had a history of failure and were already convinced that school had nothing to offer to them. Memories of my own school experience came rushing back. I knew exactly how they felt. It occurred to me that it was going to be no easy task to make this year's English class productive for them.

My classroom was on the third floor of an aging, traditional brick school building. Along the east wall, just above the waist-high bookshelves, tall windows spanned the length of the room. The morning sun flooded the room on this September day that was already promising to be sweltering. I had opened the windows to allow for some circulation, hoping that the heat would not become unbearable as the day wore on.

I walked behind my desk, laying down the book sign-out list, and picked up my copy of the literature book to begin the day's lesson. Just as I looked up, out of the corner of my eye I saw Richard hurl his book with all his strength toward the open windows. It whizzed by me, hitting the top of the bookshelf just below one of the windows and narrowly missing the unfortunate pigeon who had just perched on the window sill. Wings flapping frantically, the pigeon made a hasty retreat.

In that split second, I was carried back to my own childhood again. Everybody in my East Baltimore neighborhood, it seemed, had pigeons, including my grandmother. Whenever I was punished, which was often, I would be sent to my grandmother's. There I would spend my exile – alone for hours "talking" to her pigeons.

I had learned a lot from the pigeons.

I turned back to Richard. I could see the expectation for reproach in his eyes. Instead, I asked him, "Richard, did that pigeon have anything in her mouth?" He looked at me, totally confused by this unexpected question.

"What?" he responded.

"Did she have anything in her mouth, maybe some grass or a stick?"

He didn't know how to respond.

I said, "She might be building a nest to lay an egg."

You could have heard a pin drop in the room. All eyes were on Richard and me. I knew this was the moment that would change everything – for Richard and for the rest of the class. This was the focus we needed.

I took the opportunity and ran with it.

I told them some of the things I had learned from "talking" with pigeons. The class was riveted. I pointed to the closet in the back of the room and said, "Come over here and look."

I walked toward the closet. Richard and Dan were the first to get up. Eagerly, everybody else followed. Before I opened the closet door, I looked at the faces of these students and saw, for the first time, the innocent children hidden behind their tough exteriors.

Their curiosity was tangible. "What did the closet have to do with the pigeon?" they asked. I explained that the pigeon needed a safe and secure place to build her nest. We were going to provide that for her. Then we would watch her progress.

I opened the door and pointed to the window in the

back of the closet. "We're going to leave that open all night. Tomorrow morning we'll check and see if she came in to build her nest. Meanwhile, we're going to prepare a place in there for her to build her nest."

I grabbed a stack of old newspapers that were sitting on the bookshelf and handed them to Richard and Dan. "Pull these apart and give everybody several sheets," I told them. I balled up a sheet myself and said, "Okay, you do the same thing and let's throw these balls of newspaper in the closet for her."

Richard and Dan and their classmates dove in to the project. I could feel their energy and building excitement as they balled up sheet after sheet and threw it into the closet, creating a growing haven of crumbled newspaper.

We spent the rest of the class period building new knowledge about pigeons and building our relationships with each other. They were full of questions. They wanted to know why she might be likely to choose that closet, instead of someplace else. They wanted to know more details about how I had learned so much about pigeons. They wanted to know more about me, and in the process, they shared more about themselves and their lives.

The next morning, everybody arrived on time. They couldn't wait to open the closet door. I held them at bay. "I need just one person to check," explaining that we didn't want to scare her off.

"It's gotta be Richard," said a girl in the back of the room. "He discovered the pigeon."

Richard stood a little taller.

"No, he tried to kill the pigeon," said another classmate.

"If it's Richard's pigeon, maybe he'll behave," suggested Dan.

The class voted that Richard would be the one.

I herded everybody out in the hall. I cautioned them about making noise that might frighten the pigeon if she was, indeed, in the closet. They were tense with anticipation as Richard and I walked back into the room and approached the closet door. As I looked over my shoulder, I could see their bodies pushing for a place in the doorway, waiting for the revelation.

My hand on his shoulder, Richard looked at me tentatively. "What should I do?" Dan's insight had been right on target. Richard was actually asking me about the appropriate way to handle this. He was focused!

"Just open the door a crack and peek in." I offered. "Try not to make a sound. Once you've looked, then close the door as quietly as you can."

He put his hand on the doorknob and began to turn it slowly. We all held our breath. Richard moved in slow motion. He leaned his face toward the growing crack in the door. Not a sound came from his mouth.

In a few seconds, he turned to me wide-eyed. I could tell by the look on his face that she was there. Then he grabbed me by the arm, and dragged me back to the hallway, where the words burst out of his mouth, "She came! She came! She's in there!" The class cheered and jumped up and down with delight.

And so our interdisciplinary unit of study was born, the focus determined by the beginning of a class relationship with a pigeon. Over the next weeks, we read informational text and led discussions about pigeons. We learned that they mate for life and rear their families together. We learned that the incubation period for pigeon eggs is 17 to 19 days, and so much more. We observed and documented our observations, videotaping the habits of our pigeon friend, the laying of her egg, and the birth of her baby. We wrote poems and raps. There was not a single eighth grader in that room who didn't taste the success of lessons learned. Thank you, Richard, for giving us our focus.

> *" ... When focus is combined with other variables ..., student achievement gains are more than five times greater ..." (Reeves, 2010)*

As a firefighter and as a teacher, I have learned that focus is the foremost factor in successfully achieving the goal of both professions.

As firefighters, our focus is first saving lives. Everything we train for is strategically designed for that purpose. We rehearse our skills and tactics over and over again, so that our responses in emergency situations will be automatic. We work as a team to ensure that our efforts to save lives have the best chance of success. We reflect about our work to find ways to be more effective. Saving lives is the *WHY?* of what firefighters do, both in preparation and in professional practice. As a result there is never a question of what our focus should be. Our focus is, undeniably, to save lives.

In his book, *Focus: Elevating the Essentials to Radically Improve Student Learning* (2nd Edition, 2018), Mike Schmoker alludes to the dramatic growth in student achievement that would happen in a relatively brief amount of time if schools were to focus only on implementing "what is essential." So what is the essential focus in the profession of teaching? It can be nothing other than successful learning for every student. It is that learning that can save the lives of our future generations. The focus of teaching, like firefighting, is to save lives.

As a teacher, early on, I learned from students like Richard and his classmates that finding a way to reach them and help them learn had to be my focus. By focusing on what works to accomplish that, I could make a difference in the lives of even the most challenging students. In my year with Richard and his classmates, I saw those children learn the value of providing a safe and nurturing environment to another living being. Simply by developing their capacity to support and assure the health and welfare of a mother and baby pigeon, they learned knowledge and skills they had never encountered before. We found the instructional focus for our classroom, and they found purpose in their learning.

The value of such focus lies in that sense of purpose that permeates everything we do – firefighters and teachers, alike. In his reference to Daniel Pink's research (2009) on human motivation and performance, Douglas Reeves (2011) suggests that meaningful work is at the heart of human motivation. The implication for teachers is that a focus on saving the lives of students through education provides the impetus for "efficacy and effectiveness." The implication for students is that a focus on purpose-driven learning can propel all students forward toward positive and productive futures.

As schools are encouraged to establish their school-wide instructional focus (Palumbo and Leight, 2007), teachers will identify and implement the specific strategies within that focus for use in their classrooms. To determine what is essential for the effective learning of all of their students, teachers must rehearse the research-based strategies proven to work, respond to their students' needs with strategic and intentional actions, and ultimately reflect about the outcomes of those actions (Dunkle, 2012).

One tool for launching that process is the *Strategic and Intentional Action Strategy* template (see following page). This template provides teachers a structure for thinking about a particular challenge they are encountering with their students' learning, the research that would support their selection of a strategy to use with students, and the selection of a particular strategy for addressing the challenge.

As Jim Collins voiced in his book, *Good to Great* (2001), "The real path to greatness, it turns out, requires simplicity and diligence. It requires clarity; not instant illumination. It demands each of us to focus on what is vital – and to eliminate all of the extraneous distractions."

Teachers, like firefighters, have the potential to save lives every day. A focus on learning, whatever it takes to make that happen for each and every child, is the first step.

STRATEGIC & INTENTIONAL ACTION STRATEGY TO IGNITE FOCUS

The Challenge
Students often seem unengaged and unable or reluctant to talk about what they understand and don't understand from their reading, their experiences, and/or their thinking. As a result, the rigor of their discussions and resulting learning is compromised.

↓

The Research
Reciprocal Teaching is among Hattie's "Top Twelve" instructional strategies that research has shown have the highest impact on student learning. Also on the "Top Twelve" list, are class discussion and feedback that are integral ingredients of the process of Reciprocal Teaching. These three strategies have been proven to dramatically increase student achievement.

↓

The Action(s)
Use Reciprocal Teaching as an instructional activity for engaging students in a dialogue about what they have read, experienced, or thought about a concept or idea. Using predicting, clarifying, questioning, and summarizing strategies, students explore and build upon their understanding. (See *References*.)

↓

THUS If students seem unengaged and/or are struggling with understanding a concept, their experiences, or their reading; then the skills of predicting, clarifying, questioning, and summarizing in Reciprocal Teaching can help them construct meaning from their learning experiences and be actively engaged. For all students, the rigor of teaching and learning is increased.

References

Collins, J. (2001). *Good to great: Why some companies make the leap and others don't.* New York, NY: Harper Collins Publishers, Inc.

Dunkle, C. (2012) *Leading the common core state standards: From common sense to common practice.* Thousand Oaks, CA: Corwin, A Sage Company.

Hattie (2018). "Hattie Ranking: 252 Influences And Effect Sizes Related To Student Achievement". https://visible-learning.org/hattie-ranking-influences-effect-sizes-learning-achievement/

Firefighting death and injury data retrieved from U.S. Fire Protection Association, 2018, https://www.usfa.fema.gov/data/statistics/; National Fire Protection Association, 2018, https://www.nfpa.org/, and Fire Safety Statistics, https://www.unitypoint.org/blankchildrens/fire-statistics.aspx.

Gassenheimer, C. (2019). "Five insights on the 10th Anniversary of John Hattie's Visible Learning Research." Alabama Best Practices Center. https://aplusala.org/best-practices-center/2019/02/14/five-insights-on-the-10th-anniversary-of-john-hatties-visible-learning-research/

"Glossary of Hattie's Influences on Student Achievement." https://visible-learning.org/glossary.

Foch, F. (n.d.). *Leading thoughts: Building a community of leaders.* Leadershipnow.com. Retrieved May 6, 2014, from Leadership Now.com Web site: http://www.leadershipnow.com/passionquotes.html.

Hattie, J. (2009). *Visible learning: A synthesis of over 800 meta-analyses relating to achievement.* New York, NY: Routledge.

Hattie, J. (2015). *Visibile learning.org* https://visible-learning.org/hattie-ranking-influences-effect-sizes-learning-achievement/

Juvenile Justice Bulletin (October 2001). Washington, D.C.: Office of Juvenile Justice and Delinquency Prevention, Office of Justice Programs, U.S. Department of Justice.

Learning Policy Institute. https://learningpolicyinstitute.org/

Oczkus, L. (2018). "Chapter 1. The Fab Four: *Reciprocal Teaching Strategies*". *Reciprocal teaching at work: Powerful strategies and lessons for improving reading comprehension, 3rd Ed.* Alexandria, VA: Association of Supervision and Curriculum Development http://www.ascd.org/publications/books/118045/chapters/The-Fab-Four@-Reciprocal-Teaching-Strategies.aspx

Palumbo, J. & Leight, J. (2007). *The power of focus: More lessons learned in district and school improvement.* Bloomington, IN: Xlibris Corporation.

National Center for Education Statistics. https://nces.ed.gov/programs/coe/indicator_cgg.asp

Pink, D. H. (2009). *Drive: The surprising truth about what motivates us.* New York: Riverhead Books.

Reeves (2011). *Finding your leadership focus: What matters most for student results.* New York, NY: Teachers College Press.

Saving Lives, Inc. (2013). *Strategic and Intentional Action Strategy* template. Middle River, MD: **Life Saving Books**.

Schmoker, M. (2018). *Focus: elevating the essentials to radically improve student learning*, 2nd Edition. Alexandria, VA: ASCD.

"Teachers as Role Models." Teach.com. https://teach.com/what/teachers-change-lives/

"Teachers Change Lives." Teach.com. https://teach.com/what/teachers-change-lives/

About The Author

As the founder of *Saving Lives, Inc.* Dr. Al Thompson is passionately dedicated to motivating his audiences/readers to take action on behalf of children. In addition to his professional development work with teachers and administrators around the country, Al is an experienced keynote speaker and consultant for school and districts. He has recently published his first book in the series, *Saving Lives Through Education, Ignite Focus* which parallels his experiences as a decorated firefighter with those of a successful educator. He brings his genuine love for people, his passion for saving the lives of young people through education, and humor to his story -- inspiring audiences/readers to commit to strategic and intentional actions that focus on high performance teaching and learning experiences for all students. His unparalleled commitment to service to others is inspired by his former career as a lieutenant with the Baltimore City Fire Department.

Al initially completed his A.A. degree, in Fire Protection Technology, at Baltimore City Community College (MD). Then, after a decorated career, with the Baltimore City Fire Department as Lieutenant, he completed an undergraduate degree (B.S.) in Jurisprudence at the University of Baltimore (MD). After beginning his teaching career, he completed a Master's degree (M.S.) in Education Administration and Supervision, at Towson University (MD) while simultaneously completing coursework at Coppin University (MD), to be certified in school administration. In June 2002, he received a doctoral degree (Ed.D.) in Educational Leadership from Nova Southeastern University (FL). Through his research and dissertation, Al studied educational alternatives to ensuring high school graduation for students experiencing academic, social, and/or emotional challenges.

During his career in education, Al has served both rural and urban school districts with diverse student populations, K-12. His positions have included classroom teacher, turnaround principal, district administrator, and Leadership Coach. He has received recognition for accomplishments in program planning and staff development that focuses on improved academic opportunities for socially and economically disadvantaged students.

As can be seen in his job experiences and education, he has never shied away from challenges. From Baltimore City firefighter to urban school administrator, he has always met the challenges inherent in those positions, head-on.

Recently, he encountered a new challenge that has further motivated him to offer his support to others - he was diagnosed with Parkinson's disease. He has learned to meet this challenge head-on, as well. In 2016, he underwent deep brain stimulation surgery to control the tremors that had made it difficult to do even the most everyday sorts of tasks (e.g., feeding himself, picking up a glass of water, etc.). The surgery successfully diminished the tremors, and although he lives daily with the on-going challenges of Parkinson's Disease, the surgery has allowed him to return to managing the daily tasks of living and continuing to reach local, state, and national audiences/readers with his inspirational message. Al resides on the Chesapeake Bay in Middle River, Maryland with his wife, Beth, also an educator and the current CEO of *Saving Lives, Inc.* Al and Beth are the proud parents of two grown daughters, Becky and Sarah.

To learn more, visit: www.savinglivesinc.com

A Preview of Book 2 of the Saving Lives Through Education Series: Fuel Feedback

October, 1974
Firefighter
Baltimore City, Maryland

Finally! It was my first day on the job at the firehouse. Right out of the academy, I had been assigned to 7 Engine, the second oldest firehouse in Baltimore City. In years past, the cobblestone floors of this firehouse had helped thrust horse-drawn engines to their destination. The bell tower of this historic firehouse housed the bell from Baltimore's world-famous Lexington Market.

Assigned the nightshift, 4:00 p.m. – 6:00 a.m., I came in a little early. I was eager to put my training into action, so it was 3:30 when I walked through the door. There were three other firefighters there already, guys I had never met before. They began the "rookie razz" right away. "Go clean the poles, rookie," they hollered.

Soon, Captain Liam Billary arrived – a proud, rugged and seasoned professional – definitely "old school"! By 4:00 p.m. on the dot, two more firefighters had reported for duty. I continued to be the target of the veterans' razzing until 4:30, when we got our first call! There was a fire in a vacant building, just two blocks up on Eutaw Street. My adrenaline started to pump, and my heart felt like it was going to jump out of my chest. Immediately, the razzing stopped and each firefighter sprung into action.

To go north toward the fire site, our engine had to do a complete U-turn in front of the firehouse. We rolled out and turned in the direction of the vacant building up the street, and immediately saw smoke. It wasn't black; it wasn't brown – like I had expected it to be. Instead there was this fluffy, white cloud ahead of us. One of the guys on the engine said, "It's a mattress fire!" I thought, "What's he? Psychic?" Another firefighter nodded his head, confirming his buddy's assessment. "I can smell it!" I could smell something, but what was it? "Urine," he said off-handedly. Then I understood. Everybody else knew what to do; I tried to follow their actions and give the impression that I knew what I was doing.

We had a whole complement responding to the fire – 4 engines, 2 trucks, and the battalion chief in his car. As we pulled up, I could feel my excitement mounting; I jumped off the engine and ran around to the back and began pulling off 1½-inch hose immediately.

"Take a booster line! No need for the hose," the Captain yelled to me. "It's only a mattress!" The booster line was the red hose on a reel, attached to a 300-gallon water tank. We wouldn't have to hook that up to a hydrant. "Got it," I hollered back and began to put my air mask on. "You don't need that," the Captain said as he headed toward the vacant house without any protective equipment himself. I followed, catching up with him. I could see heavy, thick, white smoke coming from the windows of the second floor of the building. As the rookie, I could feel the Captain's protective eyes on me.

We headed up the steps as the smoke billowed down toward us. The challenge was on!

At the top of the stairs, the white smoke was dense. Hose in hand, I immediately aimed a straight stream toward the ceiling of the room to create the effect of a sprinkler head, as I had been trained. The Captain screamed at me, "Change the nozzle to 'spray,' rookie. Direct the fan of water toward the area of heaviest smoke." As I responded, he said, "Take care of it, rook! You'll be alright," and he turned and walked out and down the stairs, leaving me on my own.

Steam and smoke rolled out of the room as I directed the water according to the Captain's command. All I could see was a yellowish-white smoke. I crouched down and crawled on my knees and elbows, pulling the booster hose with me. The smoke was starting to get to me. Choking and coughing, with no mask, I saturated the room with water. I could see the fire smoldering. There were no real flames. Then I saw the source of the smoke – two mattresses, folded up against each other.

There was a rope tying the two mattresses together. I pulled a tool out of my pocket, a fire academy graduation present; it was a combination seatbelt cutter and knife. I knelt down to cut the rope as I continued spraying the mattresses with water. As I sliced on the rope, I caught a glimpse of old clothes – jeans, shoes, etc.

I turned the hose toward the window, fanning out the water to pull the smoke out and up. The smoke began to clear. I turned my focus back to the smoldering mattresses, and just then, the rope gave way. The mattresses popped open, flames erupted, and suddenly, a nauseating smell in the room overwhelmed me …

School Year, 1993 – '94
Middle School English Teacher
Baltimore City, Maryland

I was teaching in a racially charged school in Baltimore City in the early 90's. The area where the school was located was in the news continually, with reports of conflicts in the school or on the streets nearly every week.

Ann and Debbie were rising 8th graders whom I had met during the preceding school year. They were a unique pair. Ann already had set a goal for herself; she planned on becoming a teacher. Her appearance reflected that focus and self-confidence. Debbie, on the other hand, seemingly lived in the moment—often showing up at school, disheveled and appearing to be under the influence. Near the end of that summer, before beginning their 8th grade year, I would see them hanging out together on school grounds, often in the building and wandering the hallways. Suddenly, I realized that many students sought refuge in school.

When I discovered they were among the students on my class list, I decided to tap into Ann's eagerness to become a teacher and perhaps bring Debbie along for the ride. One afternoon when they were wandering around the building during those last days of summer, I stopped them in the hall to see if they might be interested in serving as peer tutors for the coming year. I explained a little about what a peer tutor does, and I offered to share with them some of the work their class would be doing from September through to Thanksgiving break. Ann jumped at the chance and actually began previewing the reading and accompanying work. Debbie was a little more hesitant, if not reluctant, to participate in the task. However, she hung around with Ann and eventually got pulled into the process. The two girls actually began completing some of the assignments I had shared with them as practice for their peer tutor responsibilities to come. Meanwhile, I began setting up my classroom for the year.

I arranged the student desks in groups of four to facilitate collaboration for a reading/writing workshop model of teaching and learning (thanks to the inspiration and guidance of Nancy Atwell, founder of the Center for Teaching and Learning and renowned educational author, widely known for her book, *In the Middle*). I had planned for each table group to have the name of a writer whose work the students would be reading during the year. (e.g., Mark Twain, Shirley Jackson, Robert Frost, Gwendolyn Brooks, etc.). So I made placards with those names on them, and Ann and Debbie helped me hang one above each of the table groups.

By the time school opened for all students at the beginning of September, my classroom was ready for action! Ann, Debbie, and I had a running start on the curriculum and instruction for the fall semester. We were all three eager to get started with the girls' peer tutoring!

Though most of my students would have easily been candidates for the girls' support, we chose Will as the first recipient of peer tutoring. Will had already failed twice according to his school records and he was approaching 16 years old. He did not have the background knowledge, vocabulary, or skill to formulate a response – or he didn't seem to think he did. Overweight, soft-spoken, and quiet; his discomfort during class was tangible. He said little and seemed embarrassed by his presence in school. Early on, I discovered that when I called his name to take attendance, he would just grunt and look away. If I called on him to respond to a question or participate in an activity, he would freeze. I could see the panic in his eyes in those moments.

When I organized the learning teams in Ann and Debbie's class, I put the girls together in a group with Will and another student. (The girls insisted on working together in their roles as peer tutors. They had recognized the "Power of 2," long before I did, apparently.)

The girls had both been supportive of Will and the other student in their table group, encouraging both to persist when they encountered difficulty with the reading or the writing assignments. Using the knowledge the girls had gained in their previewing of the curriculum in August, Ann and Debbie seemed to have an instinctive way of knowing what Will or the other student in their group needed.

One Monday, when we had been in school for 5 or 6 weeks, Ann and Debbie showed up in my classroom at 7:00 a.m., ninety minutes before class was scheduled to begin.

They had an idea that they wanted to share with me. On the preceding Friday, each of the students in the class had been assigned to prepare an oral reading of a stanza from a poem. They would be asked to present their reading aloud in class today. All the students knew that I typically called on them randomly by drawing slips with their names on them, from an old coffee can. The girls told me that they wanted me to call on Will to read his stanza first, no matter whose name I actually pulled out of the can. The girls had a plan; I trusted that plan.

When I drew the first slip, according to Ann and Debbie's plan, I ignored the print in front of me and called Will's name. I recognized that panicked look that came immediately into his eyes. He was frozen in his seat. I could feel his pain, so I backed off and said, "No worries – I'll come back to you." I turned to another student and said, "James, why don't you come up?"

And then I heard Will's voice. "No, you called my name!" Will stood up and came to the front of the class with his book. He turned and faced his classmates ...

Book 1 of the Saving Lives Through Education Series, *Ignite Focus*, reveals to readers that, like firefighters, teachers have the potential to save lives every day. A focus on learning and whatever it takes to make that happen for each and every child, is the first step.

Book 2 of the Saving Lives Through Education Series, *Fuel Feedback*, again reinforces the idea that teachers, like firefighters, are "first responders" and reveals the second step in saving students' lives through education – providing feedback that will ensure that each student learns successfully. Read this next book in the series to discover the three facets of the feedback process, integral to successful teaching and learning.

www.ingramcontent.com/pod-product-compliance
Lightning Source LLC
Chambersburg PA
CBHW070802050426
42452CB00012B/2450